EXPRESS YOURSELF

Composition Writing Prompts Workbook

Jenny Pearson

Express Yourself

Composition Writing Prompts Workbook

Jenny Pearson

Copyright © 2019 Kivett Publishing

All rights reserved, including the right to reproduce any portion of this book in any form.

Kivett Publishing

ISBN: 978-1-941691-42-7

Language Arts > Composition

Describe music that you enjoy listening to, including why you enjoy it.

_____
_____
_____
_____
_____
_____
_____
_____

Do you know the lyrics to any songs by heart? If so, write them down. If not, make up lyrics. Sing along.

_____
_____
_____
_____
_____
_____
_____
_____

Close your eyes. Imagine the aroma of a delicious meal being cooked. Describe anything about the meal, from preparing the meal to eating it.

Consider the question, "How are you?" A common yet simple response to this question is, "Fine." Describe in detail how you really feel today.

brainstorming

Generating a list of ideas relating to a specific topic or problem is called **brainstorming**.

(Note: The term 'brainstorming' is often applied to a group of people. However, in the context of creative writing, it may also be applied to an individual writer.)

One way for a writer to apply brainstorming is to write several words down on a sheet of paper. You might group related words together, but how you do it is up to you. The main goal is to generate a variety of ideas.

Problem: Describe a problem that you wish to solve.

_____
_____
_____
_____
_____
_____

Use the space below to brainstorm ideas for a solution.

Solution: Use the results of your brainstorming session to develop a solution to the problem. Describe your solution in detail.

_____
_____
_____
_____
_____
_____
_____
_____
_____
_____
_____
_____
_____
_____
_____
_____
_____
_____
_____
_____
_____

Read about a current event that interests you. Briefly summarize the event.

_____
_____
_____
_____
_____
_____
_____
_____

How do you feel about the event? Does the event impact you? If so, describe how.

_____
_____
_____
_____
_____
_____
_____
_____

What do you enjoy doing for fun?

_____
_____
_____
_____

How often do you get the opportunity to do this?

_____
_____
_____
_____

Describe what the activity is like.

_____
_____
_____
_____
_____
_____

Describe how you feel while doing this activity.

_____
_____
_____
_____
_____
_____

Name a famous inspirational person whom you would enjoy meeting.

Make a list of questions that you would like to ask this person.

What is the name of the last movie that you watched?

_____
_____
_____
_____

Critique the movie.

_____
_____
_____
_____
_____
_____
_____
_____
_____
_____
_____
_____
_____
_____
_____

Do you believe that there is a god or higher consciousness? (Answer yes, no, or not sure.)

_____
_____

Why do you believe this?

_____
_____
_____
_____
_____
_____
_____
_____
_____

List some benefits that your belief offers.

_____
_____
_____
_____
_____

Think of a piece of fruit. Don't name it in your answers.

List adjectives that describe how it looks.

_____
_____
_____

List adjectives that describe how it tastes.

_____
_____

List adjectives that describe how it smells.

_____
_____

List adjectives that describe how it feels to touch it.

_____
_____

List adjectives that describe the sound it makes when you bite it.

_____
_____

Show your answers to your friends. Were they able to guess which piece of fruit you were describing?

List words that help to describe your personality.
___
___
___
___
___

What is your strongest personality trait?
___
___

How has this strength helped you?
___
___
___
___
___

What weakness would you like to strengthen?
___
___

What can you do to improve your weakness?
___
___

Draw a picture in the space below. On the next page, write a story to go along with the picture.

simile

A **simile** makes a direct comparison between two dissimilar things, often using the word 'like' or the word 'as.'

Examples:
- My teenage brother sleeps like a baby.
- The homework assignment was easy as pie.

metaphor

A **metaphor** makes an implied comparison between two dissimilar things. The reader may need to think about a metaphor in order to make the connection.

Examples:
- My memory of last night is cloudy.
- The last quiz was a piece of cake.

Make up some examples of similes.

___

Make up some examples of metaphors.

Express Yourself

What is your favorite color? Why?

_____

_____

What is your favorite holiday? Why?

_____

_____

_____

_____

What is your favorite food? Why?

_____

_____

_____

_____

What is your favorite song? Why?

_____

_____

_____

_____

Who is your favorite athlete? Why?

_____

_____

_____

_____

Make a list of nouns that you like. A noun is a person, place, or thing.

_____
_____
_____
_____
_____

Make a list of adjectives that you like. An adjective is a word that describes a noun, like red or quiet.

_____
_____
_____
_____
_____

Make a list of verbs that you like. A verb is a word that describes action, like run or eat.

_____
_____
_____
_____
_____

List goals that you wish to accomplish in the next ten years.

_____
_____
_____
_____
_____
_____
_____
_____

List goals that you have accomplished in the last ten years.

_____
_____
_____
_____
_____
_____
_____
_____

Write a letter to yourself that you intend to read ten years in the future. What would you like to tell yourself ten years from now?

Write down your favorite quotes.

dialogue

A conversation between two (or more) people relating to a single topic is called a **dialogue**.

Example:

"The special effects in that movie were really amazing," said the son.

"True, but it didn't seem at all realistic," replied the father.

"Come on, Dad. I don't want to watch the real world. I live in that everyday. When I watch a movie, I want more excitement than life has to offer."

"I believe that the real world can be exciting. I like to immerse myself into the story. For a couple of hours, I want to feel that I'm living an exciting, but real, life."

Write a dialogue between a fictional parent and child.

Describe one of your happiest childhood memories.

Describe one of your earliest childhood memories.

Write a sentence that makes you feel happy.
_____
_____
_____

Write a sentence that makes you feel sad.
_____
_____
_____

Write a sentence that makes you feel angry.
_____
_____
_____

Write a sentence that gives you hope.
_____
_____
_____

Write a sentence that gives you fear.

Write a sentence that makes you feel jealous.

Write a sentence that makes you feel bored.

Write a sentence that makes you laugh.

Think about an upcoming election. List three issues that are important to you regarding the election.

Choose one issue. Describe in detail why this issue is important to you.

Write a poem in pairs of sentences, where the last word from each pair of sentences rhymes.

Make a family tree in the space below. If you don't wish to make the family tree for your own family, do some research on a famous family.

Try to remember a vivid dream that you once had. Describe the dream in as much detail as you can remember.

personification

Writing about an object as if it has a personality or human-like qualities is called **personification**.

Examples:
- The leaves danced in the wind.
- My computer had a heart attack last night.
- The school bell suddenly sprang to life.
- These shoes begged me to buy them.

Make up some examples of personification.

Think about a person whom you would like to interview. Who is this person?

_____
_____

What does this person do?

_____
_____
_____

Why would you like to interview this person?

_____
_____
_____

Ask a question starting with the word 'What.'

_____
_____
_____

Ask a question starting with the word 'Where.'

_____
_____
_____

Ask a question starting with the word 'When.'

Ask a question starting with the word 'Who.'

Ask a question starting with the word 'Why.'

Ask a question starting with the word 'How.'

Which place would you like to visit? Why?

_____
_____
_____
_____
_____

What is an activity that you would like to try? What interests you about it?

_____
_____
_____
_____
_____

Which food would you like to taste for the first time? Why?

_____
_____
_____
_____
_____

Who would you like to meet? Why?

_____
_____
_____
_____
_____

Which book would you like to read? What interests you about this book?

_____
_____
_____
_____
_____

How are you feeling right now? What caused you to feel this way?

_____
_____
_____
_____
_____

What is a topic that you would like to learn about?

_____

_____

Research this topic. Take notes about this topic in the space on this page and the following page.

_____
_____
_____
_____
_____
_____
_____
_____
_____
_____
_____
_____
_____
_____
_____
_____
_____
_____

What is the source of your information?

Give an example of something that makes you feel confident.

___

Give an example of something that helps you feel better when you're not content.

___

Give an example of something that helps you feel more focused, determined, and motivated.

___

Choose a medium (like talking, writing, singing, dancing, or painting) that you could use to express yourself. Write about how you like expressing yourself with this medium. Give an example.

alliteration

When multiple words in a phrase or short sentence each begin with the same sound, this is called **alliteration**. (Note that the beginning letter is usually a consonant.)

Examples:
- Just juggle the jars of jelly.
- My mother made my mittens.
- They thought that this theater cost three dollars.
- We wondered which way you would walk.

Make up some examples of alliteration.

Write down the first relevant thing that comes to mind when you read the phrase 'break a leg.'

___

Write down the first relevant thing that comes to mind when you read the phrase 'glass half full.'

___

Write down the first relevant thing that comes to mind when you read the phrase 'Mona Lisa smile.'

___

Write down the first relevant thing that comes to mind when you read the phrase 'kill them with kindness.'

___

Write down the first relevant thing that comes to mind when you read the phrase 'once upon a time.'

_____
_____
_____

Write down the first relevant thing that comes to mind when you read the phrase 'sting like a bee.'

_____
_____
_____

Write down the first relevant thing that comes to mind when you read the phrase 'laughing out loud.'

_____
_____
_____

Write down the first relevant thing that comes to mind when you read the phrase 'blind leading the blind.'

_____
_____
_____

What are your thoughts on the subject of the growing use of cell phones?

What is your opinion on the subject of bullying?

What are your thoughts on the subject of the influence of the media on self-esteem and body image?

What is your opinion on the subject of peer pressure?

Describe in simple terms how to use a hammer.

Describe in simple terms how to eat an apple.

Think of something that you know how to do very well. Provide clear instructions for how to do it that would be easy for almost anybody to understand.

(If you don't know who the person is, do a little research on them before you answer the question.)

Which words do you associate with Albert Einstein?
_____
_____

Which words do you associate with Mother Theresa?
_____
_____

Which words do you associate with Hercules?
_____
_____

Which words do you associate with Martin Luther King Jr.?
_____
_____

Which words do you associate with Joan of Arc?
_____
_____

Which words do you associate with Abraham Lincoln?
_____
_____

Which words do you associate with Oprah Winfrey?

Which words do you associate with Leonardo da Vinci?

Which words do you associate with J.K. Rowling?

Which words do you associate with Isaac Newton?

Which words do you associate with Helen Keller?

Which words do you associate with William Shakespeare?

Which words do you associate with Winston Churchill?

Choose a fairy tale. Write the title below.

Imagine that a reporter is interviewing the villain. Write down questions and answers for the interview.

Now imagine that the reporter is interviewing the protagonist. Write down questions and answers for this interview.

onomatopoeia

When a writer uses or creates a word that mimics a particular sound, this is called **onomatopoeia**.

Examples:

- The sandwich landed on the ground with a splat.
- I heard several moos and oinks when I visited the farm.
- The cat purred when I scratched her head.
- The only sound in the room was the persistent tick tock of the grandfather clock.

Make up some examples of onomatopoeia.

Give the title and author of the last book that you read.

Briefly describe the protagonist.

Briefly describe the antagonist.

Briefly describe the book's setting.

Summarize the plot.

Do you believe it's important to keep a secret? Why?

___

Is it ever okay to break a promise? If so, give an example. If not, explain.

___

Do you believe spreading a rumor is equivalent to sharing a secret? Explain.

___

Has a rumor ever been spread about you? If so, how did you feel? If not, how would you feel if it had?

___
___
___
___
___

Are rumors common in your social circles? Provide a reason for this.

___
___
___
___
___

In a social circle among teenagers where rumors are common, what could be done to reduce the rumors?

___
___
___
___
___

Doodle page: When you can't think of something to write, return to this page and draw doodles on it.

What was the last thing that made you smile? Describe the event in detail and how it made you feel.

___

When was the last time that you made someone else smile? Describe the event in detail.

___

Make a list of things that you are thankful for.

Write about an emotional issue that has bothered you. If you wish, you can make up fictional names for people and places.

imagery

The use of descriptive and figurative language that appeals to the five senses is called **imagery**. Note that similes, metaphors, personification, and onomatopoeia sometimes aid imagery (review pages 18, 34, and 56).

Examples:

- The darkness was interrupted by a sudden ball of light that was blinding like the sun.
- The soda bottle opened with a pop followed by the sound of fizz.
- It was juicy and tasted like a mix of cherry and lemon.

Make up some examples of visual imagery (color, shape, size, pattern).

_____
_____
_____
_____
_____
_____
_____
_____
_____
_____

Make up some examples of auditory imagery (pleasant sounds, noises, silence).

_____
_____
_____
_____
_____
_____

Make up some examples of tactile imagery (touch, texture, temperature, movement).

_____
_____
_____
_____
_____
_____
_____
_____
_____

Make up some examples of gustatory imagery (tastes, flavors, spiciness, savoriness).

_____
_____
_____
_____
_____
_____

Make up some examples of olfactory imagery (pleasant fragrances, unpleasant odors).

___

Make up some examples of imagery that apply similes, metaphors, personification, or onomatopoeia.

___

Create your own fantastic beast. Give it a name.

Describe what the beast looks like.

Describe what the beast does and how it behaves.

Describe an embarrassing moment that you might be willing to share with someone else.

_____
_____
_____
_____
_____
_____
_____
_____

Describe one of your best achievements.

_____
_____
_____
_____
_____
_____
_____
_____
_____
_____

Think of a meal that you would like to cook. (If you're not sure how to cook it, do a little research.)

List the ingredients. Briefly describe each ingredient.

Write down the recipe for how to prepare the meal.

Imagine eating the meal with good company. Describe this in detail, including all five senses: sight, sound, smell, taste, and touch.

Write a letter to an imaginary pen pal.

allusion

An indirect reference is called an **allusion**. (Note that the word 'allusion' is different from the word 'illusion.' The word 'illusion' refers to a false deception. A writer might make an allusion, whereas a magician might create an illusion.)

Examples:

- I'm surprised that your <u>nose isn't growing</u>. (This is an allusion to *Pinocchio*. You might say this about somebody if you suspect them of lying.)
- When they saw one another, it was as if their <u>hearts</u> had been pierced by <u>arrows</u>. (This is an allusion to Cupid's arrows. This sentence describes love at first sight.)

Make up some examples of allusions.

Think about something in the world that you would like to see change for the better. What is it?

_____
_____

Write a persuasive argument directed to somebody who has the power to do something about it.

_____
_____
_____
_____
_____
_____
_____
_____
_____
_____
_____
_____
_____
_____
_____

Describe yourself to someone who has never met you.

Describe something that looks beautiful to you.

_____
_____
_____
_____
_____
_____
_____
_____
_____
_____

Describe what inner beauty means to you.

_____
_____
_____
_____
_____
_____
_____
_____
_____
_____

Describe what it feels like to win.

_____
_____
_____
_____
_____
_____
_____

Describe what it feels like to lose.

_____
_____
_____
_____
_____
_____
_____

Describe how it feels to be a good sport after losing.

_____
_____
_____
_____
_____
_____

Use the table below to create a timeline. Enter a date (or a year) on the left, and briefly describe an event that is important to you that occurred on that date.

Imagine that you could invent any device you want. Describe one such device in detail, including what it does, how it works, and how it might be used.

If you were a superhero, what would your name be?
_____
_____

What superpower would you like to have?
_____
_____

Provide examples of what it would be like to be this superhero.
_____
_____
_____
_____
_____
_____
_____
_____
_____
_____
_____
_____
_____

Make an outline for a short story.

_____
_____
_____
_____
_____
_____
_____
_____
_____
_____
_____
_____
_____
_____
_____
_____
_____
_____
_____

(There is space to write the short story on the following two pages.)

Write a short story on this page and the next page.

Continue the short story on this page.

irony

Verbal irony is a statement where the language means the opposite of what is intended. **Irony of situation** occurs when reality is the opposite of expectations (or when actions result in an effect that is opposite to what was intended).

Examples:

- When he opened the curtains to reveal a blizzard, he said, "It's another bright sunny day." (He is using verbal irony. It may also be sarcastic.)
- The prisoner grabbed the deputy's pistol and locked the deputy in the jail. (This is irony of situation, since an audience would expect the deputy to lock the prisoner in the jail.)

Make up some examples of verbal irony.

Make up some examples of irony of situation.

Describe a style of music.

Describe a style of dancing.

Describe something that you enjoy doing on a hot summer day.

_____
_____
_____
_____
_____
_____
_____
_____
_____

Describe something that you enjoy doing on a cold winter day.

_____
_____
_____
_____
_____
_____
_____
_____
_____

Make a piece of art out of words or sentences in the space below.

Think of a positive word that is five letters long, like SUPER. Write five positive sentences, where each sentence begins with one letter from the positive word.

Compose the lyrics to a song.

Describe the music that would accompany your song.

Describe dance moves that go along with your song.

Think of an object that makes a common noise. Indicate what the object is and describe the noise.

_____
_____
_____

Think of an object that makes a common smell. Indicate what the object is and describe the smell.

_____
_____
_____

Think of a common object that has a distinct texture. Indicate what the object is and describe the texture.

_____
_____
_____

Think of a common food that has a distinct taste. Indicate what the food is and describe the taste.

_____
_____
_____

Think of a career where the workers wear a specific type of uniform.
___

Describe in detail one of the workers wearing this uniform.
___

oxymoron

An **oxymoron** combines two contradictory terms together.

Examples:
- awfully good
- deafening silence
- strangely normal
- bittersweet (compound word)

Think of oxymorons that you have heard, or try to make up your own examples. Use each oxymoron in a sentence.

Describe your greatest strengths.

___

Identify an area that you would like to improve.
Describe what you could do to improve it.

___

List things that you are looking forward to.
___

Describe positive aspects of yourself.

Describe your favorite article of clothing, including why it is your favorite.

___

Do you enjoy shopping? Why or why not?

___

Describe an event that had a significant impact on your life. How did this event change you? What did you learn from it?

Which items would you include in a time capsule?

___

Explain why you chose these items.

___

Describe an automobile that you like. What do you like about it?
___
___
___
___
___
___
___
___

Who is your favorite teacher?
___
___

Why is this your favorite teacher?
___
___
___
___
___
___
___

Think of an animal. Which animal is it?

Describe how the animal looks.

Describe noises that the animal makes.

Describe where the animal lives.

Describe how the animal behaves.

___

Mention other facts about the animal.

___

Think of a moral that you would like to convey to young children.

___

On this page and the following page, write a short story that conveys this moral.

___

Continue the short story on this page.

hyperbole

A statement that is deliberately exaggerated in order to emphasize a point is called **hyperbole**.

Examples:

- I'm so hungry I could even eat the table.
- The speech lasted for an eternity.
- He has been complaining about that nonstop.
- This homework assignment is impossible.

Make up some examples of hyperbole.

Write down your favorite jokes.

Describe some situations that have made you laugh.

Describe a fond memory that you have involving a close relative.

_____
_____
_____
_____
_____
_____
_____
_____

Describe a toy that you remember playing with as a child.

_____
_____
_____
_____
_____
_____
_____
_____

Describe a good deed that you have done.

Describe a good deed that someone has done for you.

Write a five-paragraph essay with an introduction, three body paragraphs, and a conclusion about an issue that you feel strongly about.

Continue your essay on this page.

Describe something that you learned how to do recently.

___

Describe something interesting that has happened recently.

___

Write a short article about something that you enjoy.

Write a short autobiography.

Prepare a condensed resume. What is most important?

Imagine that you are an author who is currently having an argument with his or her muse. Write down a section of this argument.

Write about a friend (past, present, or future).

utopia

A place with an idealized society is called **utopia**.

Describe the key feature of your version of utopia.

Do you believe that human civilization will ever reach a state of utopia? Why or why not?

Do you believe that human civilization will improve in the future? Why or why not?

What did you enjoy about the *Express Yourself Composition Writing Prompts Workbook*?

_____
_____
_____
_____
_____
_____
_____
_____

How did this workbook help you express yourself?

_____
_____
_____
_____
_____

Please write a review for this book at Amazon.com or BN.com. Your feedback will help other customers who are shopping for similar books. The author, Jenny Pearson, and her publishing team will appreciate the time you took to write your review. Thank you. ☺

CURSIVE HANDWRITING

It's never too late to learn cursive handwriting.

- Learn how to write the cursive alphabet.
- Practice writing words, phrases, and sentences.
- Challenge yourself to remember how to write each letter in cursive.
- Writing prompts offer additional practice.

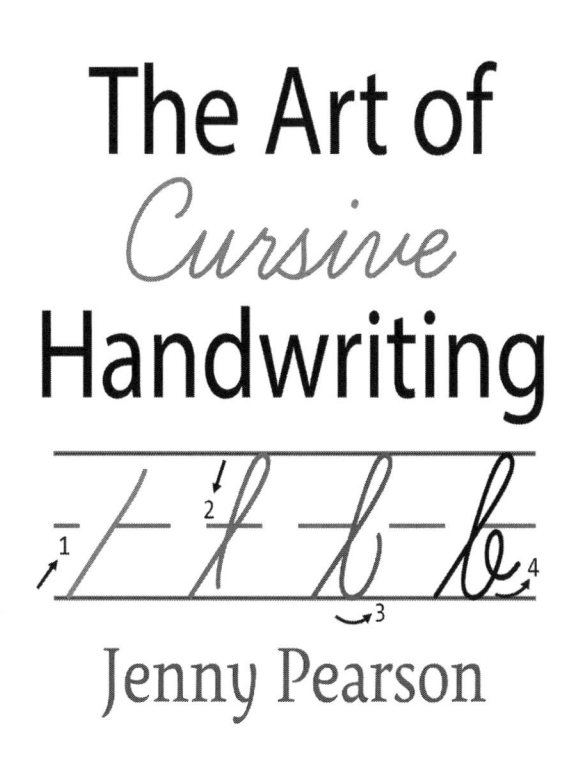

SPELLING AND PHONICS

Spelling and phonics go hand-in-hand together:

- In *The Art of Spelling*, you learn techniques for how to spell a word after you've heard it spoken.
- In *The Art of Phonics*, you learn techniques for how to pronounce a word that you see in writing.

The Art of
PHONICS

tough	through
though	thorough
thought	throughout

Jenny Pearson

The Art of
SPELLING

s	spag	spaghet
sp	spagh	spaghett
spa	spaghe	spaghetti

Jenny Pearson

COLORING BOOKS

Coloring books aren't just for kids. They are popular among teens and adults, too. Coloring provides a relaxing way to take your mind off of stress, and lets you use your creativity.

Made in the USA
Monee, IL
06 November 2022